The Forgotten Child

From Brokenness to Healing Series

by Pastor Dr. Donna Fox

Editor: Anthony Ambrogio

Cover Design: SOS Graphic Designs

Publisher: G Publishing LLC

ISBN: 978-1-7359426-0-5

Library of Congress Control Number: 2020920250

Published and Printed in the United States of America

The
Forgotten
Child

I would like to dedicate my first book to my parents Alvin and Joyce Vaughn, Jr. Without you, there would be no "me." Although I endured much as a child, I know without any doubt that you loved me unconditionally. You both desired the very best for me, and you were cheering me on, even in your absence.

Daddy, how I wish you could have stayed to see that I turned out "all right" in spite of all that I went through as a teenager and young adult and into adulthood. I said "Yes" to the call of God for both of us!

Mama, I know you did your best, and I only wish you could have lived long enough to see how God healed me from the "inside out."

I appreciate and love you both more than mere words on a paper can express. There is not a day that goes by that I don't think about you both.

I Love You Dearly

Acknowledgements

First, I want to give God All the Glory! I can do nothing without Him, He saw the best in me, and I'm so glad!

To my wonderful, devoted husband, Cornell Fox: I am nothing without you. Your unwavering love and support have brought me through so many rough times—times that I never mentioned, times when I didn't know if or how I was going to make it, times when I felt defeated and needed to be encouraged— you were there; you were there to just push me through, saying, "Let's just get through today." I am forever grateful and humbled that God loved me so much to put you in my life; I Love You and I Honor You as you walk alongside me in ministry. Thank You!

To my first-born, Terrell "Terry" Vaughn (my son-husband), my protector. Always encouraging with a voice of reason, even as a child. You have given and continue to give me a different perspective, inspiration, and strength. Thank You, for loving and respecting me through my mess (good, bad, and ugly). And, even as God has called me into "servanthood," you are still there to support, encourage and protect. As I look at the husband, father, and grandfather that you have become, I realize I must have done *something* right. I am so grateful to be able to call you "son," and I love you with every ounce of my being.

To my son in heaven, James "Jay" Kennedy Jr, I love you more than words can say. There is not a day goes by that I don't look at your picture or think about you. I didn't understand then why you were having children so rapidly at such an early age, but, now that I look back, I am so grateful for the three gifts you left me. I see you in each one of them (especially your grandchild who looks just like you). I Love You, my son.

My darling daughter, Tiffany. After having your brothers, I waited almost 10 years to have you, and I'm so grateful that I did. The enemy tried to take you from me, but God said, "Not so!" I love the confidence and boldness that you possess. I look at you and wonder what my life would have been like if I had had just a little bit of what you possess. I can't live life through you, but I'm so glad that I got to see you develop into such an amazing woman. A gorgeous (model-ready) wife, mother, and daughter. I thank you for all of your love and support. Thank you for always being there, no matter what! I am so grateful for your love as you walk with me as I fulfill my God-given assignment in Gods Peace Ministry. Love You more than words can say.

To All those who have supported and continue to support me in ministry—my Pastors, Pastor Doctors Sherome and Lady J Ivory, and my spiritual mom, Pastor Jean Glover, and to those who cover me in prayer and encouragement, Apostle and Prophetess Douglas, Apostle and Prophetess Posey, and so many others—Thank You. I could not have done it without you.

I acknowledge that, although I have often felt like the "Forgotten Child," I realize I have been "Beautifully Broken."

Foreword

As I sit here thinking about all that God has done and is doing in my life I am so amazed that I have actually put many of my doubts, shortcomings, and insecurities on paper.

As a child, I always felt like the "forgotten child." This mentality has followed me all through adulthood. Never feeling good enough, never feeling that what I thought mattered, and never desiring attention from those who had chosen to judge my past or current situations. I have always tried to stay in the background so that my secrets would not be exposed.

After many years of hurt and pain, I had built a wall that had me self-imprisoned for a long time. The fact of the matter is, even though I have written this book, I continue to work to tear walls down that were built through the years.

No, the average person would never know it. I'm good at "keeping secrets."

As you begin to read this series, "From Brokenness to Healing," I am sure that you will find yourself among the pages.

I give God all the Glory and Honor for His Healing and Delivering hand, that, by relating my many struggles and victories, I may be able to help others.

Table of Contents

Introduction

My earliest memories are of myself as a young child living on McClellan Street. I don't know why this street has stayed in my mind all of these years, but I often think about it. I think about the families that lived on McClellan with us. The Williams stayed across the street from us, and they had a lot of children, brown-skinned children. Then there were the families that lived in the four-family duplex down the street from us. That's where we played a lot. And then there was Ms. Bessie, a white lady who lived on the corner upstairs from some commercial property. She was my mom's friend, and we would take messages to her from mama, or she would hang out the window and call down to us to give mama a message. They did that a lot.

My family consisted of my father, mother, and other siblings. We also had an elderly aunt by the name of Aunt Hallie who lived with us. She was mean, and would spit brown stuff in a can. I later found out it was called "dipping snuff"—what a gross habit. I remember, when she was in her room and we tried to come in, she would chase us out with her cane, except for my brother Bobby. She loved my brother Bobby because he had to empty the "nasty can," but it was obvious she didn't like the rest of us. Bobby was welcome to come in; the rest of us had to stay clear of her and that cane. As a child, I always wondered why she didn't like us. This question would never be answered.

One particular day, while I was playing down the street with friends, the subject of race came up. I don't remember how, but I know the answer to this question sent me into an identity crisis, even as a child.

I boldly declared that I wasn't like the other kids because I was white, like Ms. Bessie. When the kids began to laugh and make fun of me, I frantically ran to my mother, hugging her by the waist. I pleaded with mama to please tell these kids that I was white. As she hugged me, she gently busted my bubble and informed me that I was just like the other kids; I was indeed black.

That day was the day that started the fight or struggle that I would have to fight even through adulthood, a subject that never seems to go away, a constant question throughout my life. I find myself constantly defending the fact that I am indeed a Black Female. My struggle exists because I am too light to be black and too dark to be white. Needless to say, my family nickname growing up was "white girl." Even to this day I will occasionally be called by this name. The sad part is I never understood the light- or dark-skinned issue.

It's one thing to be disliked by another race because

of the color of your skin, but to have to fight this battle constantly within your own race is hurtful and tiresome. You always hear from the "dark-skinned" perspective, but when was the last time you ever heard of a panel discussion dealing with the "light-skinned" perspective? Everything I have gained I worked for, from studying in school, to becoming a hard worker with a good work ethic and a character which enabled me to truly care for people, regardless of their race, creed, or financial background.

Despite popular beliefs to the contrary, I don't ever remember any opportunity afforded to me because of my skin color (but I could be wrong about this). Can you imagine how hard it is to not be accepted by either side? I never understood it, and I doubt I ever will.

This issue would be the first of many obstacles in my life. Little did I know that this would be the beginning of fear, doubt, low self-esteem and rejection, just to name a few. And to think it all started on McClellan Street when I was three or four years old.

1. Mama

My mother's name was Joyce Blanche Stewart, and she was born on April 14, 1932, to Kenneth and Ella Stewart. She was the oldest of 11 children (12, if we include Karen, who passed during infancy). The family ancestry included American Indian, Irish, African American, and Caucasian. (My mother used to tease me and say that I had the temper of an "Irishman" because I would get so easy angered). The Indian, Caucasian, and African American came from her father. I remember my great-grandfather, William Lovejoy Stewart. He was a tall, frail man who used to walk along Michigan Avenue from his home, stopping and speaking with people every step of the way. My great- grandmother was white, with very long hair that she would braid then roll up into a bun.

My mother would often tell me about us being descendants of President Andrew Jackson. According to history, he fathered many children with slave women. There is an actual group that was created to embrace and recognize their ancestry. Although he was a

US President, it brings me no joy to look back at the many injustices he brought upon the Indian and enslaved black races.

Needless to say, our family's skin color ranges from dark to "looking" white. Some even went through life passing for or identifying as a white person. This gained them access to different places and jobs that they probably would not have been able to receive if they were honest about their race, or so it's been said.

I never knew much about my grandmother's side of the family. I know she is from North Carolina and her maiden name was Cobb. My grandmother's grandfather came from Ireland, and he married a former slave. From this union, I only know of two children: my grandmother, Ella Stewart, and a sister named Bessie (I have only seen her a couple of times). Although my grandmother looked white, her sister was the total opposite, but they looked like twins.

My Mom had a beautiful relationship with her mother and honored her greatly. Grandmama was a baker, and she would make beautiful cakes—from wedding cakes to cakes with dolls in the middle of them. And she could sing and play the piano. Although I didn't inherit many particular gifts from my relatives, I believe that I did receive some of the singing and music from her and my Dad. They both played piano.

Although my mother had a loving relationship with her mother, her relationship with her father was far from that! My mother had a good/bad relationship with her father, Rev. Kenneth Stewart. I remember times when I was a young girl that we had to go to the Wayne County Jail to pick up my grandfather for driving too fast or driving drunk or for various other issues. I never remember him actually working, but he did try his hand at several businesses from owning a large car wash to power washing homes to owning a second-hand store next to his church. He always seemed angry, and I can count the times he seemed genuinely happy, but mama always seemed eager to please him. She would always say, "He still my daddy," regardless of the situation.

They often disagreed. I remember one big argument that they had. My grandparents were part of the Masons and Eastern Star. Once a month we would be dragged down to the Mason building on Detroit's east side for their regular meeting. The Masons would meet in one room, and the Eastern Star would meet in another room. At the end of the meeting they would come together to discuss what happened at the meeting, then we would have a meal.

This particular time there was a disagreement about the finances. My mother was the treasurer, and my grandfather was the leader of this particular chapter, so he wanted to take money for personal reasons, and my mother wouldn't allow it. The argument got so heated that my mother turned in all the money, books and everything else that belonged to the organization and walked away. As a little girl, I don't think I ever remember seeing my mother so upset—to the point of tears—and we never went back. She walked away and never looked back. As bad as I think the situation was, she never disrespected him but continued to bail him out again and again.

I often wonder if her relationship with him had always been so rough. She always tried to be close, but it never worked out; it wasn't long before there was another disagreement. Still, I know she loved her dad—and she loved her mom even more.

Every Saturday night was family night. Our family would all meet up at grandmama's house. All our aunts and cousins would be there. Grandmama always had a beautiful cake waiting for us when we arrived. I loved it there. Always so much love embraced us as soon as we walked through the door—genuine love, not like Granddaddy. Us kids would play and the adults would sit and talk for hours smoking cigarettes and drinking coffee. I always looked forward to going over there. Grandmama's house was also reserved for Christmas Eve as well. Same scenario, except gifts were involved. So many gifts, so exciting for us children. This custom went on for years until grandmama's health began to fail.

When I think about all the times we spent together with family, I can remember so much love but also so many secrets. Some secrets were eventually exposed as I got older, but some things were never talked about. The rule was "What goes on in my house, stays in my house." I believed that rule was started at Grandmama's house. You didn't tell or discuss, nor did you tell anyone what was going on. The family just assumed that everything would turn around for their good. But some things have to be confronted in order for real healing to begin.

I don't know what secrets Mama kept, but I have a feeling there were a lot. She never discussed her childhood except for some occasional glimpses. One that I remember was that while attending Miller High School in Detroit, she dated the legendary singer, Jackie Wilson. I also recall her telling of some incidences that happened while she was living on a farm in Petoskey, Michigan. She spoke of Grandmama shooting a black bear, and she recalled with sadness that they were forced to move back to Detroit when it was discovered that they were black and not.

I can only imagine her being the oldest of 11 children and the difficulty that may have caused even in her personal life. I know that she took the younger children under her wing because they were real close in age to my brother Lee. It still amazes me to think that my Mother and Grandmother were both pregnant at the same time, wow!. But such things probably still happen, even today.

Granddaddy played baseball in the Negro Leagues and would travel around the country to different towns to play. Baseball often caused him to travel down south and in the mid-western states. My aunt has shared with me how he would allow a couple of the children to ride to him while traveling in Michigan. However, when the Negro League games took him to other destinations the children were left for Grandmama to care for. With eleven children to feed food and resources was always in short supply. My Mother would talk about the struggles they endured while he was away playing baseball.

He always wanted his own business, from car repair shops to car washes to home improvement. He was the first person I knew who would buy houses, fix them up and then sell or rent them out. He was doing that back in the 1970s...so the practice of flipping houses has been going on for a long time.

7

My great-grandfather's name was William Lovejoy Stewart, and my mother adored him. He was a tall, thin man who (in the eyes of a young girl) looked a lot like an Indian Chief. I remember he would always be walking. He used to walk from his home to downtown Detroit, just for the sake of walking, picking up things along the way. I used to love going over to his home. He always had Cashew nuts or Pistachios, and we could have all that Mama would allow us to eat. His house was the "fireworks house" too. He had built a shed onto the back of his house, and he would lift us up to sit on the roof to watch the fireworks.

When he became sick, it was a difficult time for my mother. When she had to put him in Grace Hospital, the one thing he asked was for her to let him walk down Michigan Avenue one more time. Because of his illness, my mother tried to explain to him that he couldn't do that, and he passed away that very night. My mother was heartbroken and often wondered if she would have let him walk one last time, whether that would have made a difference. We all know that the will of God was done, but it didn't make her feel any better. I know she had many sleepless nights wrestling with her decision, knowing all that time she had no control over what God had ordained.

My Mama was the kindest person I knew. She loved her family so much that everything she did revolved around us. Even when we were children, I never remember her going out with friends or getting out of the house. She always surrounded herself with us. As we grew older and became adults, she still wanted us around, and then our children and children's children around. Every Sunday we met up at her home. By this time we had started respectively calling her "Big Ma". It didn't matter what time you came, but you were automatically expected to be there. The Sunday dinners were amazing, and the meals always consisted of two meats. I will never know how she managed it, but it goes to show you the dedication and love she had for her family. As I look back, I pray that someday I will be half the woman she was, but I don't think they exist anymore. Not like Big Ma; she was one of a kind. I am not naïve, and I know that she was not without fault, but to me, she was the Greatest Mom ever! Oh, how I miss her presence.

My mother and father dated while my mother was in high school. They had planned to be married afterwards. Unfortunately, their plans would be spoiled by my Mama's father. On the day of their wedding, my mother's father went and spoke to my father. After their conversation, my dad didn't show up for the wedding. They actually found him hiding under the bed; isn't that crazy? The wedding didn't go forward and they both went their separate ways for a few years.

My father never spoke of what was said to him; that is something that he took to his grave. I often wonder what my grandfather could have said that would cause my father to act like that. I can only imagine it had to be something awfully powerful.

As my mom moved on with her life, she ended up in another relationship, her first marriage. Although she never spoke about it, she did conceive and give birth to two sons Lee Stewart (her maiden name), and Bobby Barnes (her married name). At some point she moved to Milwaukee with her husband, who was very abusive, and the family had to go to Milwaukee and move her back to Detroit, for the safety of her and her children. When Mama was returned to Detroit, my brother Lee was around five and Bobby was around three years old. It didn't take long before her and Daddy would eventually be back together and finally married.

She was intelligent and a very hard worker. As a young girl, I remember my mom moving from a Human Resources/Receptionist position at Alden Nursing Home on Jefferson Avenue to become a Nursing Home Administrator. She employed most of her family (including my dad). I remember going to visit my grandmother while she was at work. She used to work in the kitchen preparing meals for the residents, and sometimes we got to go visit.

Later, Mama became Administrator over several Nursing Homes and Home for the Aged facilities. She was my first boss and allowed me to work in the kitchen for Longfellow Nursing Home and Boulevard Home for the Aged. When my father became ill, she took on another job at Reid's Pharmacy to help ends meet.

Little did Mama or any of us know that, in her jobs at the nursing home, she was working for one of the big crime bosses who had close ties with Jimmy Hoffa. His name of Leonard Schultz. When Jimmy Hoffa disappeared, one facility was closed down by the state. A few years later, the Home for the Aged closed down, and Mama began to work at the pharmacy full time. She also got me a job with her, and I began my pharmacy career that would last over 25 years until I transferred from Veterans Administration Hospital to the United States Postal Service. It all started with her having the faith in me to believe that I could do the job.

From the outset, my mom and dad seemed like the perfect couple. I remember them working as waiters at these big socialite parties, and they would bring the food ideas home. Every New Year's Day, we would have a big party for both sides of the family. The table would be spread, and the drinks would be flowing. It still brings me joy when I think about all the joy and happiness our families shared together. When Daddy got sick, it abruptly stopped. The party was over!

There were always children around our house. Not only did my parents have five children of their own, but we always had other children living with us—aunts staying with us trying to kick drug addiction, cousins living with us because of addictions. My cousin Diana (DeeBay) stayed with us the most. She was close to my age and my sister's age. Whenever her mother would go on a drinking binge, she would come over and go to school with us.

Then we had our other cousins Kay and Moe, my mother's sister Marlene's children. My mom and their grandmother (Nana) entered into a custody battle over the children. My mom eventually lost the fight, and they were raised by their grandmother Zora. It broke my mother's heart because she always felt that they would be happier living with her.

During the time of my father's illness, they adopted my little sister, Betty. She was actually born to my mother's sister Dee, but, because of Dee's drug abuse, she was unable to care for Betty. She would bring her over for my brother Bobby to babysit and wouldn't come back for weeks. Eventually Mama and

Daddy made it legal; they would adopt her and change her name.

And one more would come: my little brother KJ. My mother's brother Kenneth (Kenny) had gotten sick and was trying to care for his son alone. Seeing his struggle, my mom asked him to come to our house with his son so that he could have some help in caring for the boy. By this time, my siblings and I were all adults and had children around the same age as Little KJ. After Uncle Kenney's passing, Mama continued to raise KJ as her own. Her love and compassion for children was unlimited. She was always fighting to make sure children were taken care of. She loved all children. From those in the neighborhood to our family members, no child would be unloved or uncared for.

She was a faithful wife even to the end. After my dad passed, we would spend our summer at the cemetery making sure his grave was full of flowers. See, my dad had given instructions that he didn't want to be buried in Lincoln Memorial Cemetery or out in "no man's land" where all the other "blacks" were buried. Nope, he wanted to be buried in the city, and she made sure that he was.

His death was devastating in more than just a physical sense. All the family gatherings stopped. All the coming by to see how you were doing ceased. My mom was left alone to fend for herself with her children. I don't remember any of my aunts coming by to offer a hand. No uncle came by to help with my brother. My heart aches just knowing all that she endured and that no one seemed to care. I can't say that they didn't, but, if they did, it wasn't shown—not to her anyway. It was like she became a "black sheep" to my dad's family. We lived on a busy street, and I can remember times that they would ride by and not even speak. Was it her fault that my dad passed away, or was there nothing left to gain? Where did everybody go? The one thing I remember is, whenever they did call my mom because *they* needed help, Joyce showed up! Always there for everyone else, but who really was there for her?

Although she did look for love again, it was years before she finally met and fell in love with Mr. Raymond Price. For the first time in a long time, I actually saw my mother happy, and it lasted for many years. Little did we know that, because of his alcohol abuse and high blood pressure, Raymond had developed kidney disease. Like so many African American men, he would eventually end up on dialysis, and he too died. Once again, Mama was heartbroken and alone.

So she returned immersing herself into caring for her children and grandchildren. Through no fault of her own, she was forced to raise my sister's six children while my sister went in and out of the prison system. I say "forced" because there was no way my mother was going to allow anyone else to care for them. No one could do it better than she could.

Because I was a single mother, Mama even allowed my sons to stay with them through the school year so that I could work (and because I too found myself in an abusive relationship; more on that later). I believe the children gave her a sense of purpose and pride. Knowing that she was needed, wanted, and loved. Everyone needs to feel loved!

I know my mother suffered many heartbreaks and disappointments, but she never acknowledged the pain. After the loss of my father and brother, I only remember her shedding a tear one time for both. On each occasion, we were sitting on the front porch together, alone, as we often were. We talked for a while about my dad, and, as the tear dropped, I got up and went and got a tissue. It's funny, but the same thing happened when we lost Butch. One tear dropped, I got up to get the tissue, and we never spoke about it again. She was an expert at hiding the pain, and she taught me well.

I often wonder if she developed Lewey Body Disease Dementia as a way of escaping reality. When you have gone through so much heartache, so much pain, finding an escape route doesn't sound so bad.

When choosing mates, we must be careful because the soul ties can be detrimental to our lives for years to come. Not only does the choice affect our lives—the people that surround us are affected as well. I have no doubt that many of the things my mother endured, I endured too. Call them

17

generational curses or whatever, but, as I look back over her life and think about my own life, I see so many similarities. I just wish we could have talked about it. I wish that she would have trusted me enough to confide in me, or someone, anybody! The hurt, pain, and disappointment could not have been good for her, mentally.

The philosophy that says "Do what I say not what I do" or "Whatever goes on in my house stays in my house" may seem good at the time, but it causes us to be locked up in our emotions. Locked up with fear, doubt, unbelief, shame, and guilt. This causes pain that only God can heal and deliver us from.

2. Daddy

My father was Alvin Vaughn Jr, born November 20, 1926 to Alvin and Jessie Vaughn in Frankfort, KY. He was the second oldest of seven children (the oldest son), and he was the kind of father every little girl dreams of. Strong yet tender hearted, intelligent and full of wisdom.

My earliest memories of Daddy were when he used to work at Detroit Bank and Trust as a janitor, and sometimes on Saturday he would let us go to work with him. He even let us empty some of the trash cans. Just being with him was exciting.

Daddy was a tall, handsome man. He stood about 6' 3" and was big in stature. He was "bigger than life" to me. And he loved his family

My dad worked his way up from a janitor to a Supervisor of the Computer Room. He was one of the few blacks who actually functioned in a managerial position (back then it was unheard of) and especially dealing with computers. My mother said that she believed, when his company said they could no longer hold his position, he lost hope because he was a very proud man. It had been a long road, and she believed he just gave up after that.

My father passed away when I was 15 years old, but I feel I lost him years before he physically left this earth due to his diagnosis of colon/rectal cancer. How I wish I could have gotten to know my father more intimately. How I wish I could have known him as the man that he was and not just the "father" that I pictured him to be.

Not only was he book smart but street smart as well, and I loved to listen to him talk to my older cousins about life and being a man. I remember him saying, "All I want to do is live long enough to see my kids become grown," but it wasn't in God's plan.

He had a "larger-than-life" laugh, and he loved life. His laughter would fill up the room. He used to like sitcoms; his favorites were *All in the Family* and *Sanford and Son*. He would actually LOL (laugh out loud) from his belly. He had such a "robust" laugh. When he laughed, you had to laugh with him; it was contagious. I loved his sense of humor; he was fun, but he kept things in order.

Daddy loved gospel music, and we could count on being awakened every Saturday or Sunday morning to James Cleveland, Mahalia Jackson, or Aretha Franklin. I would lie in my bed and just listen to the music flowing through the house. I also took my time getting out of bed because I knew it was house-cleaning time. This was the time set aside every week for the house to be cleaned from top to bottom.

He was the disciplinarian of our household. He was very neat and preferred order. He taught us how to clean and organize. I remember that he awakened me late one night after he returned home from work to have me wash dishes that we had neglected to do. When you have a large family, there is always something to be cleaned, dusted, mopped, or polished, and he made sure the work was done to "the highest standards."

Funny how the things we thought were "foolish" as children we end up doing as adults. My sister and I shared a bedroom, and I remember at least once a month, either Mama or Daddy would come into our room to check things out. The closet was our hiding place all month, so, by the time they came in, the closet would be full of stuff that we just threw in there. They would just start pulling stuff out of the closet, and it would take hours for us to clean it up. As I look back, I realize that it would have been so much easier to do it right the first time. We never understood it until we became grown and had to train our own children the same way.

Providing household chores was done on Saturday our Sundays usually started out with gospel music and then Daddy was on his way out. He loved to dress well and wear cologne. He would always smell so good (in fact, that's what he called all of his cologne: "smell good").

Then he would be on his way to one or more of his sisters' houses to drink and hang out. By the time he came back home, he was so drunk that one of my older brothers would have to go get him out of the car. They would be so angry and I would be scared.

On one of his escapades, I remember him coming home and hiding his car in the garage. The police came to our house and found the car in the garage. I guess, while he was drunk, he had hit someone's car and then tried to hide the evidence. When he woke up that morning, his face had been bruised. When I asked him what happened, he told me the "sidewalk jumped up and slapped me in the face." That was his way of saying he was drunk and fell. Such a great sense of humor. Always making me laugh.

He used to joke that his car knew its way home, and, sure enough, seems like as soon as he pulled up in front of the house, he would fall asleep. While my brothers would have to get him out of the car, I would stay hidden or out of sight because I didn't like seeing him like that. It made my larger-than-life Daddy seem so small, and I didn't want to see him hurt.

My Dad taught us that when we were in public, we represented the family. He taught us how to dress and carry ourselves and to always be a lady. I remember, when we started smoking (at a very young age), he used to allow us to smoke at home only. He said that "ladies" didn't smoke in public.

My Daddy was the best cook I knew. He could cook anything! He was the family beautician as well. Every week, one of his sisters was at our house or he was at their home cutting, pressing, and curling hair.

When my sister was born, because she looked so much like my Aunt Butch (yeah, that was my aunt's nick name), she spent a lot of time at her house—so much so that people actually thought that she was her daughter. It was during one of the "hair appointments" that a neighbor came in and asked my aunt where "her daughter" was at? My dad became furious and explained to this person that that was his "damn" daughter, and he took my sister home and wouldn't let her go back. I could just hear him saying those words with an expression of indignation on his face. I'm sure it was hilarious, but I know he was so serious. He had had enough of my sister not being at home. That scenario ended abruptly, forever! He had such a way with words, I know it was an uncomfortable situation for the neighbor, but he and his sister probably laughed about it later.

He actually gave me my first haircut. My hair was long and thick, and I used to wear to ponytails (one on each side of my head), and I hated them. People would tease me and pull them and say, "Giddy-up, horsey," with my hair. One day Daddy finally gave in to my constant nagging and finally cut my hair. At the age of 12 or 13, I no longer had those big "Do Do" braids. My mom was furious when she came home and found out that he finally gave in to my request. I was excited and grateful, and we would laugh later about the incident.

He said what he meant, and he meant what he said. Daddy didn't play. The one and only whipping I remember ever getting came from Daddy. He told us not to leave the house, but I made the mistake of listening to my older sister, Ellen, who said that we could sneak two doors down to our friend Gloria's house. Well, Daddy got back early from the barber shop and we ended up getting a whipping—

or, at least, the three of us younger ones got it. Stern but fair. I loved him so much. I actually adored him.

His personality was so big. Even when he cursed, it would be like a lullaby. He had a way of putting words together that just flowed.

He didn't mention much about his childhood, but I knew that he and his dad did not have a good relationship. He respected him as his father, but there wasn't really a relationship there. As my dad was getting ready to graduate high school, his father refused to buy him long pants to wear to the graduation and insisted that he wear knee-length pants. Needless to say, my father did not participate in the graduation ceremonies and enlisted in the Air Force instead. I've seen pictures of my dad in his uniform—young, wise, and so handsome.

I was told that the reason he and his father didn't get along was because my dad was "light skinned," whereas all the other children were darker like my grandad, with the exception of one of my aunts, who was lighter but not as light as my dad. How sad that even in our families we have issues about our skin complexion. Ridiculous but true!

He loved his mother greatly, and I remember going over on some Saturday mornings. She would cook us waffles (we only ate them at her house). I know that my granddad was abusive to my grandmother, and my dad would go to check on her (the Saturday-morning visits), always slipping a little money to her. She died when I was young, so I don't remember much about her except that she was white, beautiful, and had long hair.

When we came over, she would sit in her picture window and let us comb her hair while she fell asleep. When she passed away, I remember the hurt that I saw on my father's face. I had never seen him like that. I don't know if he was crying or not, but, even at a young age, I could see the pain in his face. So I cried for him.

My dad became ill when I was about 11 or 12 years old, and he passed away when I was 15 (two months shy of my 16th birthday). Just didn't seem fair, and I would find myself in

27

some dark places as a result of not knowing about grief or how to properly grieve. Many mistakes were made as a result.

He was gone too soon.

3. Sibling Rivalry

During my mother's first marriage, she bore two sons, Lee and Bobby. When my mother married my father, they together had three more children. My sister Ellen is one year and one day older than me; I m the middle child, and my brother, Li'l Bro is one year and one month younger than me. (All siblings' names have been disguised out of respect for their privacy.)

My Mom got pregnant one more time but lost the baby; it was a boy! After that she had a hysterectomy (one of those secrets that was never talked about). In those times, a woman's inability to have children was an embarrassment, and I believe Mama was embarrassed.

The fact that we three younger ones were born at all is a miracle from God. My father had to have surgery when he was 17 years old and was told that he would not be able to have children. It came as quite a surprise when my mother became pregnant with my sister. My mother said that it was a very difficult time for her until my sister was born looking so much like my aunt(my father's sister). Because of that resemblance, they named Ellen after my aunt and my grandmother, just to discover later that she was named entirely after my aunt. Their first, middle, and last names were the same. I often wonder if her resemblance and her name played a role in her gravitating to my father's side of the family more than my mother's. Anyway, after he saw my sister and how much she looked like my aunt, I guess my father was totally convinced that he could have children. My younger brother and I (me first) followed right behind her.

In my family, we never described each other as step-brother or half-sister. It was always brother or sister. That's how we were raised. Although my older brothers were not my father's biological sons, he raised them as his own.

I don't know when my brothers found out that my dad wasn't their dad or if they always knew. I didn't find out until my teen years, but it never made a difference to me. They were just my brothers.

My oldest brother, Lee, was very handsome. He used to hang out with my younger aunts, and they all became addicted to heroin at a young age. I remember giving him my lunch money because he would be hurting so bad. I didn't understand what he was going through, but it hurt me to see him hurting, so every week I would give him my weekly lunch money.

He was always in trouble at home or with the police. My dad used to work afternoons, so Lee would wait for him to go to sleep and steal his car, steal money, and just do different things to bring confusion to the house. Many arguments went on about what he had done or didn't do. Now that I look back on it, I believe he was always rebellious and a self-described "black sheep of the family"; his own foolishness caused great pain to our family.

My mother tried everything to help him; Vocational school, counseling—anything she could think of—but nothing worked. I never knew what the real reason for his troubles were. Was it because of not knowing his father or succumbing to peer pressure? He had many demons within, and nothing ever seemed to help. I believe that getting high was an escape for him because he was not strong enough to deal with "his" reality.

As mentioned, he always described himself as the "black sheep of the family." Where did that come from? I only remember my dad trying to be a dad to him, but it was a love that he would often reject. I know my dad didn't fall for the foolishness as so many others did; could that be it? Because I was one of the younger children, I may never know the answer.

Somehow, he manipulated an Army Recruiter and was allowed to join the Army when he was underage. When he found out he was being dispatched to Vietnam, he told the truth about his age and was sent back home with the privilege of being able to return once he became legally old enough to enlist. So, he did!

Once the war was over, he went back into the Army and received an Honorable Discharge, but still he always seemed troubled. His honorable discharge allowed him to go into a Carpentry Apprenticeship Program, where he was really good. I remember going with Mama to pick him up when he was working, building large houses. He was good with his hands and could build anything.

He had a great sense of fashion, style, and class and was a smooth talker. He married Marsha Griffin, and they began to try to build a life together. His marriage lasted for a while, but it was turbulent. I remember spending a lot of time with him and Marsha, and there were always arguments. Loud and abusive arguments. Fortunately, Marsha was a strong woman and walked away from the marriage.

He would later meet Jackie. She too was a sweet girl, and she really loved my brother, but he couldn't love her because he didn't know how to love himself. To this union, my niece, Lala Stewart was born; she was an adorable baby and I know he fell madly in love with his daughter. Fortunately for Jackie, she mustered up enough strength to walk away as well.

He inflicted a lot of pain on both of these women, but I do believe that he honestly loved them, (or tried to). They were smart, intelligent, beautiful women who thought that they could love him enough to change him. Unfortunately, that's something that only God would have been able to do!

As I said, he was a very handsome guy who dressed and danced very well. He had style, and a flamboyant lifestyle to match. Women were attracted to him instantly, and he could just about get any woman he wanted. Some were smart enough to run, and others had to walk (away).

He became a drug dealer and was successful for a long time until he began to like his product more than his clients. Needless to say, he became addicted again—this time to crack cocaine, and it was downhill from there. My brother, Lee was killed in March 1987. My mother couldn't bear the thought of having to identify him at the morgue, so I was the one who had to go. That is a task that no family should have to go through. Oh, the pain! I just wish that his time here on earth would have been a little easier and happier.

My brother Bobby, got in trouble a lot, too, but he was respectful. He was a gang banger and would always be fighting. He joined or maybe even created a gang called the BMR's (Black Militant Revolutionaries) or something like that. He always had a chip on his shoulder—why, I don't know. He used to fight all the time, and, when I asked him about it, he had no real answer.

I remember he begged my mom to buy him a blue-jean jacket and when she did he cut the sleeves off of it and painted a "big black fist" on the back of the jacket, proclaiming that he was a member of the BMR's. My mom was furious.

I remember when Detroit had the 1967 riots and there were Army tanks driving down our street. My mother had told him not to leave off of the porch, but, because he had just received a new bike with the new-style handlebars and banana seat, he just had to ride it. The soldiers pointed their weapon at him and told him to get his black behind on the porch, and I have never seen him so scared. He stayed on the porch for the remaining days of the riot.

Oh, then there was that time when we went to Chicago to visit some of my father's cousins. They lived on the south side of Chicago, and everyone told Bobby to stay in front of the house. Since Bobby always felt that he was bigger and tougher than anyone around, he decided instead to walk to the corner store. Before anyone knew what was going on, Bobby was being chased back to the house. This time he couldn't come out of the house until we were returning home.

He was always into something. He was not home much but always hanging out in the streets. He and Lee used to fight a lot. During one particular fight, Bobby chased Lee all through the neighborhood My mom had gone grocery shopping, and they ended up at the supermarket where she was shopping. I can only imagine the embarrassment that must have caused her.

Bobby was athletic and liked to box. He used to box with Jim Ingram (who was a Detroit boxing promoter as well as a radio personality), but Bobby wanted to do things his way, so that didn't last long. The opportunities were there, but he didn't take advantage of them. He would later join the Marines and spend time in Okinawa, Japan. Bobby boxed in the Marine Corps and had a very impressive track record.

He and my Dad had a special bond, and I believe, during my Dad's, final days, he was trying to hold on to see Bobby one more time. Unfortunately, it didn't work out. When Bobby returned home, he was bitter because he was unable to get home to see Daddy again but those are just my thoughts. Bobby came home mad at the world and was ready to take it out on anybody!

See, when they train people to become Marines, they train them to kill, but, when they discharge them, they never "deprogram" them to come back to society. Every Marine I know came home with issues. I may be wrong, but I am speaking "my truth" as to what I have observed. They never return to the place they were before entering into the Marine Corps. So, in 1977, Bobby found himself serving a natural-life prison sentence. The unfortunate thing is that he has a son, Little Bobby, and grandchildren that he has never been able to see outside of the prison system.

Currently, his case is being studied by some law students at University of Michigan, and I believe there may be an opportunity for him to be released one day!

I do believe that prison saved his life, although, even after going to prison, he succumbed to the pressures of prison life and joined gangs and things of that nature while in prison. His beginning years in prison were hard ones, composed of solitary confinement, loss of visiting privileges, and other issues. However, I thank God that now he has repented for his sins and accepted Jesus Christ as his Lord and Savior. He even ministers to me now! Even after all these years, I still have a strong relationship with my brother, talking weekly and keeping him up to date on our family events. The one thing that I promised my mother was that I would look out for our family, so I continue to send him care packages and phone money just like my mom would do. Regardless of what has happened in his life, we are still family, and he's my brother, and I love him to life.

My sister, Ellen. All I ever wanted was to have a real relationship with my sister. But, despite being born from the same mother and father, we are as different as night and day. I don't know why; I can't explain it. We have always tried to be close, but the differences in our lives have been there for as long as I can remember.

I was busy in school trying to maintain my Honor Roll status, and she was barely making it. I wanted to do different things, and she wanted to do nothing. I wanted to keep our room clean, and she didn't want to clean up. She liked cooking, and I liked washing dishes. I didn't want to be noticed, and she demanded attention. Total Opposites—and, in this case, opposites don't attract.

Since she was my sister, I tried several times to confide in Ellen, always to my detriment. At a young age, I had learned to keep secrets, and I always wanted to be able to share them with someone. Unfortunately, whenever she would get upset with me, she told; she told every secret I ever told her. All it took was for her to get mad at you, and it was over. The Lord said "vengeance is mine," but, if you crossed Ellen, vengeance belonged to her.

I was 11 years old when I started my menstrual cycle. (I whispered the news to Ellen, and, by the time I got to school that morning, everyone else knew about it). I had no idea what was happening to my body, but I felt dirty, not knowing that this was a part of becoming a woman. Then to have everyone at school tease me about something that I didn't understand just made matters worse. I felt betrayed, ashamed and heartbroken.

This incident marked just the beginning of her betrayals or vengeful acts. There was more to come. Ellen didn't care who got hurt when she blabbed. Some of my secrets that Ellen told not only hurt me but caused pain to others as well. The one thing I can say is that she didn't discriminate; *no one* was safe from her wrath.

Ellen does have a heart of gold but she marches to a different beat; hers. She is a lot like my father's side of the family, and—not that it's a put down, but—we could never seem to find that common ground. She was always close to my father's sisters: Aunt Butch, whom she's named after, and Aunt Louise (who passed away years ago). Aunt

Butch even had insurance policies on which she designated Ellen as her beneficiary. The closest I got to anything remotely like that is I was promised that, if I got all "A's" on my report card I could pick out anything I wanted from the Sears catalog. So, I got the A's and had to wait almost a year for the red coat that I picked out. I was accepted but never developed that same type of relationship with them as Ellen did.

I wasn't really close to my mom's side of the family either. Our family was, on the one side, "poverty mentality" and, on the other side, "bogie mentality," and I didn't fit in with either side. Ellen just seemed to fit in everywhere. Everyone knows her; everyone loves her with all of her flaws.

Both sides of my family had members involved in illegal activity, mainly drug dealing. My brother once described it like this: The Stewarts talked about it but the Vaughn's did it. Why, I don't know. Different worlds, I guess.

She was always the "street smart" one while I was naïve. I thought everybody was good people, but she could see right through them. I always wanted to be with her, but it was as if she never wanted me around (I was Miss Goody Two Shoes or something). Still, she has always been a big supporter—as long as I don't get too close, because she doesn't want to hear what I'm going to say. She can see "greatness" in me but won't allow herself the same grace to acknowledge that there is "greatness" in her as well.

As a child growing up, I may have only had two or three fights in my lifetime, and they usually revolved around Ellen. I remember one fight vividly. Ellen was fighting "Big Judy" who used to live across the street from us on French Road. Judy was a big girl, heavy set, and I saw she was getting the best of Ellen, so I decided to help my sister. When I came to Ellen's aid, she took off, leaving me to fight Big Judy by myself.

Back in those days, we had an alley behind our houses, and the garbage cans would be stacked up along the fence behind our house. That girl threw me all over those garbage cans, and, all the while, Ellen was in the house watching. I believe she received a whipping for that one, but it taught me a lesson: fight your own battles.

While we were attending Joy Junior High School, I was informed by my guidance counselor that I should go to Southeastern High School for the Summer because, if I returned to Joy in the Fall, they were going to expel me because my sister had been selling joints (marijuana) at school. I didn't even know what a joint was, but Ellen's actions caused me to go to high school ahead of my friends, so no graduation for me. Again, isolated and alone! My friends were still in junior high school while I started down a path of going to Summer school every year. Why not? I didn't have anything else to do, and I wouldn't have to stay home and deal with all the "secrets."

Despite our lives being so different, I know that if I get into a pinch, Ellen's got me. For example, when we were young and lived together, we both were struggling to the point that we didn't have food to feed our children. She would go to the grocery store (with no money) and come home with enough food to feed our five children. That was the first I heard of "don't ask, don't tell," but she made sure we ate. When I had my back surgery, I couldn't have asked for a better caregiver. She was right there! But let her get back in those streets, and it's like she's a different person.

She has been through many struggles in her life as well and I am sure that there were many incidents while we were growing up that caused her to be the way that she is. Even now, as a grown woman, she still carries the baggage of a painful childhood: many disappointments and frustrations that have never been dealt with, which have caused her to live a life of substance abuse.

My sister has spent time in the prison system, which cost her relationship with her children. Her oldest child (her only daughter) and her youngest son had always been raised by my mother. During her daughter's infancy, she was always with my mom and me. However, Ellen had five other children (boys) as well. Unfortunately, she didn't have a positive impact on them either. My mother raised them all while Ellen was in and out of jail until she finally maxed out. Finally free without any parole.

I think she still tries to make up for the mistakes she has made with them. What she doesn't realize is that she can't fix it; only God can. She has to learn how to love herself first, then she will be able to love her children. How I wish I could help her!

Our relationship as adults has been just as turbulent as when we were children. I remember her accusing me one time that I didn't want her and her kids to have anything from my mother. I didn't really understand what she was saying, but, not long afterwards, I found out that my mother's bank accounts had been tampered with. It wasn't about me; all I did was care for my mother—but who in their right mind could treat their mother this way? (More on that later.). Here I go, that forgotten child that no one sees or includes. On my own again!

One thing I know for sure is that Ellen does love the Lord and supports me in ministry to the extent that she is able to do so. She pushes me beyond my comfort zone, but I can't depend on her to be there. She may show up from time to time. I had to come to realize that she is giving me all that she has to give, and for that I am grateful.

My brother, Li'l Bro is the youngest of my father's children. He has had many issues in his life—most of them as a result of losing our dad at a young age. He was the one who acted out or rebelled the most once Daddy was gone. It's unfortunate that there was no male representative who could come to his rescue.

One of the few times I remember my younger brother getting in trouble with my dad was when he skipped school. All three of us went to Hutchinson Elementary school, and, on this particular day, I just so happened to ask one of his friends where my brother was. He informed me that my brother hadn't come to school that day. So, I rushed home, thinking that my brother was sick. Little did I know that he had skipped school with some of his other friends. When he got home from supposedly being in school, he got tore up. I felt so bad for him, but I didn't know! I thought he was at home sick. I can't remember another time when he tried that again. At least, not while Daddy was alive.

Every boy needs a man in his life. My older brothers were off doing their own thing. My father had been close to a couple of my Aunt's husbands, but they never came to nurture Li'l Bro, to take him fishing or anything. We had a couple of neighborhood dads who took him under their wing, but, by that time, he was out stealing cars, running with the wrong crowd, and just making bad decisions.

He even caught a major case, but—praise God for good lawyers and money—he was able to walk away free. I am sure that, through the years, he has suffered, but he suffered in silence. Not really voicing his pain or disappointments. Trying to work it out on his own.

He got married to his childhood sweetheart and they stayed together for many years. As young people do, they had their turbulent times as well trying to be grown but young at the same time. Whenever he worked, he always had good positions, and he too was someone that everyone liked. He always gained favor from his employers and people in general.

Unfortunately, he got into the drug game too. Not only did he get into the game, but he introduced many of the young men in our family to the game. This caused most of our sons to catch drug cases. I don't know if he asked them or they asked him, but it did none of them any favors. Years later, those mistakes that were made at 17 and 18 years old are still on their police records as felony crimes.

I don't know what happened to our relationship, or maybe it has always been like this. We used to be very close when we were young and we were struggling through relationships together. Then, as time went on, we seemed to go our separate ways. I was very close to his first wife, Denise Bonner-Vaugh, because we practically grew up together. She was a teenager when they first met, and I had just had my oldest son, Terry.

Li'l Bro always wanted to borrow my car so he would volunteer to take Terry with him. He had Terry with him so often that Denise thought my son actually belonged to Li'l Bro. She was so convinced that she made him bring her to meet me so she could hear it from me that Terry was indeed my son. This started a lifelong friendship or sisterhood. With all of us being young, we went through a lot together and grew into adulthood. Although Li'l Bro and Denise eventually divorced, she and I remained close until her untimely death in 2019.

The one thing that I can truly say I regret is that my continued friendship with Denise caused a wedge between his current wife and me. I often wonder what has been said that would cause us to not develop a relationship. I love her because he loves her. If he likes it, then I love it. They have been married for many years now, and I still desire a relationship with them both. I don't know what I did or didn't do. But I have enough love in my heart to be able to have loved Denise and to develop a relationship and love for her as well. It saddens me that, through all these years, the opportunity is just presenting itself for us to become friends, and I'm so grateful to God for the shift.

When people know that they are doing things that may be considered wrong, they have a tendency to separate themselves from those whom they think may say something that they don't want to hear. And, yes, my brother has done some things that were not right, but that's between him and God. I just wish we could have that relationship that used to be. Was I too judgmental? If so, I apologize. Could it be that I'm too saved? I know life happens, but do families have to become separated because of it?

It's interesting because, at one point, I was never invited or included in their barbecues or fish fries. I don't know if it was intentional or accidental, just an oversight. Maybe it's me, but I always feel excluded. It's like I'm not wanted around or something. I have nieces and nephews with whom I don't have a relationship—why? Did I do something or say something wrong? How do you have a big family get-together and not make sure your sister knows what's going on? Is it jealousy or selfishness? Again, here I am feeling like a forgotten child (even as an adult)!

Either way, this used to really bother me, but I have come to accept that this is our "relationship." I pray that there was nothing that I have done to cause or bring harm to him or his wife, for I love them both. I just wonder what lies or misconceptions have been told that I will probably never get to set straight. I have learned to give it to God and rest in him. Can't please everyone. It's really unfortunate.

One thing for sure is I thank God that, before my mother made her transition, she was able to see or hear of Li'l Bro dedicating his life to Christ. God is able to change your life around if you let him. So, now, instead of making a living selling drugs, he and his wife have become property owners, and I wish nothing but great success for the both of them.

4. The Forgotten Child (Me, Myself and I)

During my youth, I just wanted to make mama and Daddy proud. So, I did all the "right" things. Worked hard at school, stayed on the Honor Roll, and always had good citizenship. See, if I did everything that was expected of me, I wouldn't cause any trouble, and the focus would be off of me and would stay on my brothers and sister. They always had enough trouble going on that I didn't want to add to the worries that Mama and Daddy already were dealing with.

Being the fourth out of five children, I was always lacking attention. My brother Lee was seven years older than me. Bobby was four years older, so they seemed to be doing different things from us younger ones. Since my mother's two older children were from a previous marriage, this made me the middle child of my mother and father.

In elementary school, I began to play instruments. I wanted to play the flute from the beginning, but Mama was convinced that it would make my teeth "poke" out, so I had to play the violin for two years until I could convince her to let me play the flute. I played the flute all through high school, I sang in the school choir, I was on the dance team in high school, as well. I only remember my mother coming to one recital.

I stayed active in school because at least there I did get some attention. People noticed me! At home I was always quiet, reading a book, doing homework, or playing my flute. Nobody noticed because I wasn't a problem. I always felt alone even in a home with five children and two adults.

My dad always worked afternoons or midnight shifts, and my mother was always working, so they were too busy to notice or to participate in the activities that I was involved in. In high school, I became President of the Afro Club (one of the biggest accomplishments in high school), and still they never said "congratulations" or "I'm proud of you"—nothing. They just came to expect certain things from Donna, and, as long as their expectations were met, I got little to no attention. I don't fault them at all;

they were doing the best that they knew how to do. They just didn't understand that, just because I "seemed" to have everything together, I was a mess on the inside.

Since my mom and dad both worked, to many people we were the "ideal" family. Mama worked during the week, so she usually tried to catch up on housework on the weekend. A lot of times, to get us out of her hair, she would have a male family friend named "Slim" take me and all the other kids to the Admiral Theater on Saturday afternoon. To go to the show was a big deal, and we were always anxious to go.

That's where the molestation began. There was no penetration, but the fondling allowed me to experience the gratification of the touch. While all the other kids were seated in front of us or 'way up in front (where he'd let them sit if they were good), I was always made to sit in the back, next to him. I didn't really understand what was going on, but I knew it was something that wasn't supposed to happen. But I didn't want to get myself in trouble or cause trouble in the family. It had to be my fault, and this had to be my punishment. I can't say why I felt like it was my fault, but I was convinced that it had to be; otherwise, it would have happened to my sister and my cousin, but it didn't. I think I felt like I was being punished because it felt good (even though I knew it was wrong). This went on for almost a year before it abruptly stopped. To this day I don't know why it stopped, but I was grateful that it did.

I never told anyone about this. Mostly because of shame but also because I didn't want anyone to think differently of me. Nor did I want my dad to get in trouble. If I said anything, I was scared of what my dad or older brothers would do, so I kept silent. Unfortunately, this pattern followed me for way too many years. Silence is not always "golden." But it can become a trap or a cage that entraps us mentally and physically for years until the hand of God delivers us.

My father had cousins in Chicago, Raleigh and Prissy, that he and my mom were really close to. Raleigh was very quiet and Prissy was the total opposite. They were big drinkers and would drink from the time we got there until the time we left. At their house, we always dressed for dinner and ate at a well-dressed dinner table. The china would be out—crystal glasses, the works.

The sad part is that this too was a place for secrets. As I got older, when Uncle Raleigh would get good and drunk, he would often try to catch me up in the kitchen (as I washed dishes) and kiss me or feel on my body. Again, just another secret to keep. I must have done something wrong; why me? Was my dress too short, or did I indicate in some way that I was available or open to abuse? Again, I never told. Although my parents and our cousins have passed on, this is the first time that I have ever shared this information. I guess it's my way of screaming "ME TOO" even though they are no longer alive.

It was during one of these visits that I became sick and began to vomit. My mother and Prissy began to ask me about my periods and, come to think of it. I hadn't had one. They immediately made me some "ginger tea"; this was guaranteed to bring my period on. If it didn't come, then I must be pregnant. When we got home, my mother monitored me again for a couple of weeks.

Unfortunately, their suspicions were correct, pregnant, and not even in the eighth grade yet. Since my mother was in the medical field, she was able to convince one of the doctors that *she* was pregnant, and he gave her the medication to cause a miscarriage.

All I remember is the pain; it hurt so bad. When I tried to tell my mother how bad the pain was, her response was, "It would be a lot worse having a baby; deal with it," and she stopped speaking to me. All I could do is curl up in a ball and cry. It hurt so bad, not just physically but emotionally as well. Mama was relieved when I told her I passed a huge blood clot. I don't know how long Mama not speaking to me but it seemed like an eternity. We were very close and she was all I had. I can still hear me screaming from within, calling Mama! Mama I need you, Mama help me. Although, I had always felt alone, this was different. This time I knew I was alone.

It is only now that I am dealing with the fact that—call it what you want—that was my baby whom I was too young and too immature to handle. It still hurts! Because I was so desperate for love—needing it, seeking it—

when a boy told me he loved me, I believed him. How stupid could I be? Not stupid, desperate! Another secret to hold on to.

Here's the other thing that's one of the best-kept secrets: sexual abuse was happening in my own home, too. At different times, my older brother would take me and my sister into our parents' bedroom and fondle us. He didn't bother me much because I always cried, but I remember him messing with my sister a lot. So, was this the way it was supposed to go? Boys always messing with girls? See, back in those days we didn't talk about it. "What was done in Mama's house stayed in Mama's house." This went on for a while until the "Big Fight."

One day there was a big argument at my house between my mother and father. It had something to do with my sister, and I'm pretty sure "the secret" had been revealed. I remember my oldest brother locking himself in his room, and he wouldn't come out.

My older brother had been in and out of youth-counseling centers. I remember visiting him at the Hawthorne Center for Youth, but I never remember my dad going with us to visit. We would ride with Mama, and it would always seem so far away. The majority of the times when we left, Mama would ride home in silence and in tears. I hated him for causing my mama so much pain. What happened? She was never crying before she went to see him.

I never knew what he was diagnosed with, but I'm pretty sure he was bi-polar or manic depressive. I vaguely remember a couple of time he threatened to commit suicide, but I knew he wasn't going to do it.

The fight between Mama and Daddy got so bad that they called my brother's social worker to come out to the house. Her name was Smitty, and she was always so pretty and loving. I believe she was a friend of my mother's, but, after that night, we never saw Smitty again. I believe she actually moved out of the city. I never knew what happened, but I knew it was because of the fight and my brother.

After this, our house was never the same. Mama and Daddy weren't the same. They seemed different. They didn't laugh together anymore, and they just kind of went through the motions. Mama went to work and came home and attended to us. Daddy went to work and came home and attended to us. No more family vacations, no more going out to dinner as a family. Life as we knew it changed, and, once again, I retreated to my "silent place" within myself. Trying to be seen but not heard, the invisible child.

I was so vulnerable. My insides were screaming "Can somebody please love me for *me*? Can you see me? I have real hurt, doubts and fears. I'm not all right!" So I focused on being away from the house as much as possible. At school, at least, I had people who talked to me. At school, at least, I had people that pretended to be my friends. At school, at least, I didn't feel ignored. My safe place where no one knew how I felt, no one knew what I was thinking or what I desired. Nor did anyone seem to care. SO MANY SECRETS.

I believe that all of the issues that I had to deal with as an adult began here. The obstacles that I would have to overcome as a born-again believer started here. The "forgotten-child" aspect of my existence created low self-esteem, shyness, or quietness. Depression and anxiety started here. This is where I wouldn't allow people to get too close to me. The wall had been built, and I wasn't letting anyone in. Why? Because I didn't want them to know my flaws; I didn't want to expose the ugly truth that I was sexually promiscuous just to get attention.

The funny thing is, while I was having all that sex, none of it was enjoyable. It was simply wanting someone to want me. Looking for love in all the wrong places.

This place in my life is where I began to have problems with other girls because of my skin color and the texture of my hair. It's ridiculous to think that people will not like you just because of these things, but it's the truth. So many times, I just wanted to be accepted and be friends with other girls, but it never really happened. During my junior high school years, I found myself hanging out with the wrong crowd just so I could be accepted. We were fighting, sleeping around, and hanging out in the streets. Years later I saw one of my "hang-out" friends, and she was in a wheelchair because of a stroke—too young. I thank God I was able to pull myself away before I got totally lost in that world.

You would never know what I have been through because everything I have endured I always endured in secret. I was trained to keep secrets, and I hid them well. Even now, I only release what the Holy Spirit has directed me to release. But you should know that there is so much more than what meets the eye. See, I don't look like what I have been through, and for that I am eternally grateful.

5. The Diagnosis

During this stage in my life, puberty began! Oh, my goodness. Talk about an emotional rollercoaster! Since my sexual side had already been explored, it was easy for me— being 11 years old and not understanding what sex or that feeling was all about—to look to duplicate that feeling.

I had been a chunky kid but I caught the flu one year and lost a lot of weight. Now this chunky kid began to develop. I had boobs and hips and was shapely—not realizing that this new shape would bring about a lot of undesirable attention. Besides, it was nice that people were now noticing me. It felt good!

Mama and Daddy were still working like crazy and were both going their separate ways. Mama was a workaholic and only seemed happy at work, and Daddy was working and drinking. I had a friend named Edwina Johnson, and she had a brother who was about 15 or 16. His name was Marty, and he liked me a lot (or so I thought). Actually, it was my *body* that he liked a lot, but I wouldn't realize that until later. As we would fool around, he taught me how to kiss, and he kept trying to go further, but I wouldn't let him.

Eventually I did lose my virginity to him—not because I wanted to but because I felt sorry for him. See, he told me that if I didn't let him do it to me, it would cause him pain in his stomach. I didn't know what he was talking about, but I didn't want to hurt him or cause him pain, so I let him have me—not even realizing what I was doing and that the innocence that I lost could never be regained.

I remember sitting on a curb with my sister and a friend, and I began to ask them about what it meant for a man to "come" and what "coming" meant. They laughed at me because I had let him do this to me out of ignorance. Again, I retreated!

When I was 11 years old, my father was going in and out of the hospital. Of course, I didn't think too much of it at the time. I didn't know enough to be concerned. However, the Lord gave me a dream, and in this dream, I was able to see the path my father was getting ready to take. He was diagnosed with colon/rectal cancer and would have to wear a colostomy bag. As I sat in his hospital room, I began to tell my mother and father about this dream. Little did I know that the dream was actually going to come true, but it would change my family's life forever. I felt so bad because I made a joke out of this bag that people had to poo poo into. I didn't know that this would become our reality.

Back then I blamed the dream on *déjå vu*, but it was actually a gift from God. I didn't realize that, even as a young child, the prophetic anointing was upon my life. I would often find myself in scenarios that I had seen before— from going into a store and seeing a friend to playing hopscotch and knowing how the game would turn out. It was all a coincidence until I began to accept the call on my life.

All of a sudden, our lives changed. Instead of coming home from school to do homework, we were coming home to cook dinner. My father would be back and forth into the hospital for chemo treatments, and my mother would be right by his side. They became united again! My mom would work all day and be at the hospital in the evenings. I thank God that she showed me how to care for the sick; she was my greatest example.

6. The Abuse (Molestation)

On the other hand, it left us at home alone a lot. More and more, boys were paying me more attention. So I became sexually promiscuous, looking for love in all the wrong places. It never made me feel good. In fact, I felt like crap, but somebody wanted to be around me, and that meant more than the self-inflicted hurt and disappointment I felt in my heart.

As people began to talk and spread rumors about me, again I retreated within myself. I cared, and it did hurt, but I couldn't show it. So, I isolated myself socially and emotionally; that way it wouldn't hurt so bad, I thought.

I remember one incident where I went to spend the night with a friend. Her boyfriend liked me and lied to me, telling me my friend was over to his house. When I got there, I found out he had lied. By the time I realized he had lied, my friend and some other girls showed up at his house. Once they found out I was at his house, he manipulated me and told me that if I didn't allow him to have sex with me, he was going to let them in to jump on me. Oh, I felt so bad and confused. All I wanted to do was to tell my friend that it wasn't my fault, that he'd lied to me.

The lies and manipulation that I experienced caused me much heartache, and I had no one to tell. So I retreated within again. The emptiness that I felt began to feel normal. Lost, alone, and afraid because I didn't know (this person that I had become), nor did I like her. How do you not like yourself?

Another incident happened when I was supposed to be babysitting for a lady down the street from me. Her brother who stayed with her was supposed to go out with them but made up some excuse to come back to her house. Once he came back, he tried to force himself on me, and I left the house and left him to watch the children.

Since I wasn't babysitting and didn't want to go home, I met up with a girlfriend, and we decided to try and get into a nightclub that everybody had been talking about. Once we got there, we met up with the cousin of my current boyfriend (the one I was waiting for to come home from the Marines). He was at the bar, and he talked the guy there into letting us in.

My girlfriend ended up leaving the club with a guy she met there. Alone, I agreed to let my boyfriend's cousin take me to his house. I endured a long night of sexual abuse before he finally allowed me to leave and I had to walk home.

As I was walking home around 5:00 a.m., a nice gentleman pulled up and convinced me to allow him to take me home. I remember him telling me that he had girls of his own, and he was afraid to leave me on the street. He even let me hold on to his wallet until he took me home. I was afraid, ashamed, and cold so I agreed. After the night I had just experienced I just needed to get home.

This gentleman walked me to the door and explained to my father that he had picked me up on the Chrysler service drive. I told my dad I had been raped and by whom. He took me to the hospital, and they performed an exam on me. They did verify that I had been sexually assaulted but that I was not a virgin. My dad was crushed! The pain that was in his eye was almost unbearable. He didn't speak to me for what seemed like months.

Being raped didn't count for anything because back then the general attitude was "it was your fault for putting yourself in that situation," so no charges were ever filed. I broke both my mother and father's heart, and the only way I could deal with it was to run back to my safe place, within. The pain was so great, too much for me to handle. I was so ashamed, embarrassed, and disgraced, and I had no one to tell.

7. Molestation in the Church

The sad part was the abuse didn't just happen in the neighborhood; it was happening at church as well. I adored my mother and, wherever she went, I wanted to be with her. My mother and I started attending a certain Pastor's church every Sunday (I won't bother to mention his name; he's been dead for years). Our church normally would have two services, so I would stay at the church while my mother would visit my father at the hospital.

But what was actually happening was this: while my mother was at the hospital I was at the hotel with the Pastor. He had an armor bearer who would take me to our meeting place, and afterwards I would receive my money. I actually became a "teenage prostitute," unwillingly, not really realizing it. I just wanted the money. I'm sure I wasn't the only one he and his armor bearer had done this to; it seemed to come too easy to the both of them.

As I reflect about the things in my past, I become emotional thinking about the many young girls that have been caught up in sex trafficking (it could have been me). I have come to understand that even in my darkest places, God still had His hand on me.

My sister, Ellen, began to ask me where was I getting all this money from and I decided to tell her my secret. I never told her from whom but that I was getting it from church. She promised not to tell, but—guess what—she told! It tore my mother apart. I could see the hurt in her eyes, but I couldn't tell her that her beloved Pastor was sexually abusing me. So, I kept quiet and waited for the storm to pass. I thank God that my dad never found out about this, for my dad had great respect for this Pastor as well. Even while he was in a comatose state right before his death, when the Pastor walked into the room, my father opened his eyes and greeted him, then went back to sleep. Surely, the knowledge of what the Pastor had been doing would have caused him to pass even sooner.

Needless to say, we stopped going to church and it would be years before Mama would return back to the Body of Christ. Not that she didn't love the Lord, but she had been wounded by someone she thought she could trust (even though she never knew exactly who it was). I believe that she thought it was the armor bearer, and I was fine letting her believe that.

Funny, years later while working at the VA Hospital, I had an opportunity to see this Pastor again. His words to me were, "Now we can have a relationship legally." I wanted to scream at him, "We never had a 'relationship.' *You abused me!*", but I kept silent, let him speak, and walked away with tears rolling down my face, never to speak with him again. When I found out he had died, I felt nothing— no sympathy, no concern. Nothing!

Yes, I have forgiven him, knowing that he would have to give an account to God for the things he had done. I wish there had been a "Me Too" movement back then but wonder, if there had, if I would have had the courage to stand up.

8. Teenage Motherhood

When I was 15, my dad passed away on August 23, 1975, two months shy of my 16th birthday. When most girls were celebrating turning "16," I was mourning the loss of my dad. When I returned to school in the Fall, I rebelled. I would walk in one door and go out the back door. School, which had been my escape, was now my prison. By this time, I was smoking weed and partying. It took not graduating in January 1976 for me to regain my sanity and refocus. So, I graduated in June at the age of 16 and, shortly afterwards I became pregnant. Pregnant and ashamed.

My true first love was tall and handsome (and all the girls in the neighborhood wanted him). He was five years older than me, and I felt I had really found love. I had always been mature for my age, so, by the age of 14, I had become engaged to this "wonderful man." DeWayne Smith (that was his name) proposed and I accepted, ring and all, and we were going to be married as soon as I was old enough.

My father was so upset that he wouldn't even discuss it nor look at the ring, and my mother never said a word. No "congratulations" or "maybe you should wait"—nothing but silence.

DeWayne was in the Marine Corps, and I waited faithfully on him to return home. Every time he had a trip home, we talked about our future and how we would be able to travel the world while he made a career in the Marine Corps. This was exciting to me because it would give me an opportunity to start my life over again. It would have given me a fresh start with people who didn't know me or my past. No one would be able to judge me. My life had changed, and I no longer wanted to be with anyone but him.

By the time I became pregnant, we had already been engaged for two years. Unfortunately, DeWayne no longer wanted to stay in the Marine Corps but decided to be discharged to live his life, and that he did. his plans changed, and he wanted to come home and live his life, and that he did.

While I was pregnant, he decided that he wanted to date other people. I was so desperate and in love with this man that I told him it was all right if he wanted to see other women; I just wanted to be a part of his life. Big mistake! I would watch him drive down the street with other women in the car while I was carrying his baby. I think I just wanted to be wanted, especially being pregnant.

I went through my pregnancy basically alone with the help of our mothers but not him. No companionship, no dinners, no back rubs, nothing. I just wanted him to be a part of my life and the pregnancy, but it seemed that, the more I gave, the more he took. It's ironic that he was the one who helped me to recover from all of the hurt that I had experienced, and then he delivered such a crushing blow that I didn't know if I could recover. This set me up for even more isolation and hurt. It wasn't supposed to be like this. Both my mother and his mother tried to get me to get out of the house or see other people, but I couldn't. I loved him so much—all I wanted was for him to spend time with me. This time, not only did I retreat but I became bitter.

After our son was born, we tried to get back together, but too much had happened. He would come and stay up with me through the night to watch our son, but it wasn't the same. I didn't feel the same about him because I had a child to care for now. It wasn't about me. I took full responsibility for the child I had just given birth to, and I wasn't going to let him or anyone else stop me from caring for my son.

By this time, he was working at the Post Office and thought he was on top of the world but didn't want to pay child support. He wouldn't even buy diapers, so, to get back at him, I told him, "If you can't pay child support, then you can't see my son."

I eventually moved to the other side of town so that the only access he had to my son was when Terry would be at my mother's house. What foolishness. So many wounded women feel this way, but it's not right. A child needs both parents, regardless of whether they can contribute or not. Thus, instead of getting back at him I set myself up for a lot of heartache and drama that I really didn't need.

My bitterness, which made me not allow him to see my son, proved to be a bad decision on my part, and, unfortunately, it would go on for years. My son was in elementary school before he found out who his biological father was. Although Terry knew DeWayne, he didn't know that he was the father (he was under the impression that my husband, the father to my second son, was also his father). I had planned on telling him, but it just wasn't that important to me at the time.

Terry had been acting out at school and DeWayne decided to go up to the school and reprimand him. That's how Terry found out who his father really was. I was so angry when I found out what had happened that I told DeWayne, "If you ever touch my son again, I will shoot you," and I meant every word I said. And, yes, I did carry a weapon. The hurt that I caused him and my son was not worth the price that was paid. God's grace allowed them to have a relationship, but, sadly, it wasn't because of any decisions that I personally made.

Revenge hurts, and it usually ends up hurting the very ones we are trying to protect. If I could do it all over again, I would have done things differently. Not that Terry's father would have acted any differently, but secrets would not have inflicted so much pain on us all.

At the urging of my mother, I married a man whom I had only known for less than six months. He had asked me to marry him, and I first told him no and suggested that we just live together. But, after learning that my mother approved of his proposal, I agreed (still reluctantly). He was already 10 years older than me and much more experienced in the world that I was. I always felt older than my actual age, so the difference in age was not a big deal for me. In fact, I welcomed a more mature man, someone who knew what he wanted out of life. What I didn't know was that he had been in and out of the prison system, and was a heroin addict. Outside of my brother Lee, I never actually knew a real drug addict. Lee didn't count because he was just my brother.

At the suggestion of my mother, we were married on July 27, 1977, the same day my brother was sentenced to "mandatory life" in prison. Why, I still don't know. Was it to distract from the hurt of losing another person in our family? Although Bobby wasn't dead, he would never come back home. Was it to ease the hurt and pain in my mother's eyes? How much more could she take? She had just lost her husband less than two years before.

To prove to him and myself that I was actually in love with this man, I became pregnant with my second child in October 1977, the same month and year that my grandmother died. Another loss and devastation. So, by the time that I was 18, I had two children by two different men *and* a dope-addict husband. I didn't know that the need for drugs would be greater than anyone or anything. I didn't know that he would steal our very last to supply his habit. I didn't know that this marriage would turn physically abusive before our first anniversary. Little did I know I was in way over my head, and I didn't know how to get out.

My second son, Jay, had asthma really bad, and was in and out of the hospital often. I became over protective of him because of his illness and the relationship that I had with his father. See, I needed Jay to know how much I loved him, and I never regretted having him even though my intentions for getting pregnant may not have been totally right. I know his father did some things that were not right during my pregnancy. I often wonder if that is what caused my son to struggle so much, both as a child and then as a young man, dying at the age of 21 years old.

Before I knew better, I wondered if "the sins of the father carried over to my son" because of the way Jay died? What gives me comfort is knowing that Jay had accepted Jesus Christ as his Lord and Savior and that he had a relationship with the Father. While at my son's funeral, another mother comforted me by telling me, "Donna, at least you know where your son is. My son died, and I know he killed a couple of people." That put many things into perspective for me.

I am eternally grateful for his life, as well as the lives of my older son, Terry, and my daughter, Tiffany. I Love you both with all of my heart.

To My Readers

In order for us to become completely healed, we have to be completely honest with ourselves first. This book was intended to help me in my journey of healing, and, while I intended it for myself, I believe that it can help someone else.

For many of us have had to live our lives with "secret" sins of our past. Things that we didn't want to tell anyone about because we were embarrassed or ashamed or because the memories of those sins were just too painful. However, healing can't begin until we deal with our realities.

Wounds run deep; roots run deep, but revisiting those hurting places allows the healing to begin. While I had to go back and revisit many hurtful areas in my life, it is only when we get to the root of our problems that we can be totally free.

However, traveling back to the "root of the matter" has brought a sense of healing and freedom that I have yet to fully recognize. I pray that, as time goes on, my heart will continue to be healed from the inside out.

Writing this book has caused me to look back over my life—the good, bad and ugly. I have struggled to complete this assignment because I didn't want to face or feel the pain that I have repressed for so many years. However, I have come to understand that it's only through Brokenness that I can truly become Totally Healed. Yes, I have been "Beautifully Broken".

I Say A Little Prayer for YOU

Lord Jesus, we Thank You for being a Loving and Forgiving God. Thank You for Loving and Forgiving us even when we didn't or couldn't Love or Forgive ourselves.

I lift up every child that may have ever felt "Forgotten," even in the midst of family. I pray for every "Forgotten Child" that has made a bad decision from a place of hurt, anger, disappointment, or innocence. I lift up every adult that have yet to revisit the pains of childhood, as I encourage them to do so. I pray that God will bring restoration to your life and you will live a life that is full of the blessings of the Lord.

Lord, search our hearts, and, if you find anything that's not pleasing onto you, please remove it now in Jesus' Name. Let our heart desire be to please you, removing all the hindrances out of our lives. Help us to forgive others in the same manner in which you have forgiven us. Lord, you know us better than we know ourselves, and we need your healing hand to touch, heal, and set us free today.

Lord, Thank You for becoming alive in our hearts and minds today. Fill us with a desire to be Ambassador's of Christ, here on the earth in Jesus' Name.

Amen

Coming Soon:

Book 2: Beautifully Broken
(Brokenness to Healing Series)

www.ingramcontent.com/pod-product-compliance
Lightning Source LLC
LaVergne TN
LVHW092324080426
835508LV00039B/746